Contents

WARNING: Contains buzzwords!

So what's the buzz with bees?	3
To be a bee	4
Honeybees	4
Bumblebees	4
Do bees have knees?	5
A closer look	6
Killer bees?	7
Who's who in the hive	8
One bee to rule them all	8
Up the workers!	11
Drone on	12
A hive of activity	15
Home sweet home	15
Baby boom	16
Wax works	16
Shape shifters	16
Some like it hot	17
Baby it's cold outside	17
Flower power	18
Food glorious food	18
Tell 'em about the honey mummy	18
Will you waggle dance with me?	20
Making a beeline	20
Sniffer bees go down a bomb	21
The sting in the tail	22
Warning - swarming!	23
Rain, rain go away	24
Bee bounty	25
Honey	25
Mead	25
Royal Jelly	26
Bee bread	26
Beeswax	27
Harvesting the honey	28
Smoke screen	29
Bees are an endangered species!	30
How YOU can help	31
Bee recipes	32
Honey muffins	32
'Honeycomb'	32
Honey ice-cream	32
Honey pancakes	33
Honey milkshake	33
Honey mustard salad dressing	33
Lip balm	34
Body moisturiser cream	34
Beeswax candles	34
More information	35
Acknowledgements	35
Bibliography/Photo credits	35

So what's the buzz with bees?

Sometimes you hear them before you see them. You may even be scared of them. But the more you know about bees, the more you can appreciate these unique insects and how they provide us humans with much more than just honey!

This book is all about bees, and mostly about honeybees. It's full of fascinating facts and insights into their amazing world, where nobody sleeps, everyone has a job to do and all work hard for the benefit of the community - a perfect society in miniature! It's got some great pictures, too, which help you see what these magical creatures look like close up.

I hope you get a buzz out of reading this book... I certainly got one out of writing it!

Martyn Barr

To be a bee

Bee-lieve it or not, there are over 25,000 different types of bee (OK... no more bee jokes!). The largest bee is 40mm long. The smallest is only 2mm long. You probably wouldn't mind being stung by that one!

Above: how the world's smallest and largest bees would look side by side (not actual species).

Bees can be black, brown, or banded with white, yellow or orange stripes. All bees are covered with hair, but some are hairier (and scarier!) than others.

Right: a honeybee in flight.
Top right: bumblebees tend to be larger and 'furrier' than honeybees.

Honeybees

Honeybees live in the wild and are also taken and kept in specially-built hives looked after by beekeepers.

Honeybees are often considered to be the highest form of insect life. They live in a well organised community or colony that does not need to hibernate. They produce honey and store it in a wax honeycomb that they build.

Many wild bees don't make much honey or beeswax but all help pollinate our plants and crops.

Bumblebees

Bumblebees are 'furrier' than honeybees and live in much smaller colonies. Only the queen hibernates and survives the winter. In the spring she looks for an old mouse or vole hole and makes a nest there out of leaves and moss. She builds wax cells and incubates her young rather like a bird does. When her first babies hatch and begin to fly the queen usually stays in the hive to produce more young. Bumblebees only make a small amount of honey which they store in a special cell shaped like a cup.

Buzzwords: *Victorians called bumblebees humble bees... and Dumbledore is old English for a bumblebee!*

Do bees have knees?

'The bee's knees' is a phrase we use to describe 'the best'. Although bees have legs with joints like any other insect they don't have knee caps, so I guess they don't really have knees!

A closer look

A bee's body is made up of three parts: a head, a thorax and an abdomen.

A bee has a large and a small wing on each side. They hook together to form one big pair of wings and unhook for easy folding when not flying.

A bee has two large 'compound' eyes made up of lots of tiny eyes joined together. It also has three smaller 'ocelli' eyes in the centre of its head which are used to sense light.

A bee has a sharp point at the end of its tail that it uses to sting its enemies.

A bee uses its two antennae to feel, taste and smell.

A bee has a long, straw-like tongue called a proboscis that it uses to suck up food.

Like all insects, bees have six legs. The back pair have stiff hairs to hold pollen when flying from flower to flower. The front pair have special slots which the bee uses to help clean its antennae.

Killer bees?

In 1956, African honeybees were brought to Brazil and mated with local bees to create a new breed of bee capable of producing more honey. Unfortunately, these new Africanised honeybees (AHBs) turned out to be very aggressive. That's why they were nicknamed 'killer' bees. You won't find AHBs in this country – they live in South America, Central America, eastern Mexico and in the southern states of the USA.

AHBs look like normal honeybees, but act a lot differently! They chase their enemies for longer distances and tend to gang up, stinging in large numbers. A single sting from an AHB is no more harmful than any other bee sting, but when someone is stung many times it can be very dangerous.

Buzzwords: *The Romans used beehive 'bombs', catapulting them into enemy camps to create panic... and pain!*

Who's who in the hive

There are three types of honeybee in a hive: a queen, thousands of female workers and hundreds of male drones.

One bee to rule them all

The queen is really just an egg-laying 'machine'. She only mates on one or two flights with a dozen or so male drone bees, but that's enough to enable her to lay eggs for the rest of her life... around 3–5 years!

During April and May the queen can lay an egg every 20 seconds, day and night. That's over 2,000 eggs a day... more than her own body weight!

There are three types of wax cell used for rearing eggs in the hive. In the smallest cells (5mm in diameter) the queen lays fertilised eggs, which in 21 days produce female worker bees. In larger cells (7mm diameter) the queen lays unfertilised eggs, which in 24 days produce male drone bees. A very special cell that looks a bit like a peanut pod and points downwards is used to rear the eggs that will produce new queens.

The younger bees feed the growing queens with a protein-rich creamy food called Royal Jelly (which is also fed to young worker bees but in much smaller amounts). Eight days after laying, the first queen's cell is capped with wax. When this happens the old queen usually leaves the hive with the older bees, creating a swarm.

Eight days after her cell has been capped the new queen emerges from her cell. Sometimes she leads a swarm from the hive to find a new home. If the new queen stays, she makes sure no other queen can compete with her by stinging all her sisters to death in their wax cells!

Bees only allow one queen in the hive and every queen has her own special 'perfume'. This reassures the bees that the queen is with them and that all is well in the hive. Bees are very sensitive to this perfume – or pheromone – and the 'personality' of the hive can change if a beekeeper swaps an old queen for a new one.

Left: a queen's cell is quite different from normal egg cells.

Buzzwords: *The queen bee used to be called the king bee... until microscopes enabled scientists to see the queen in minute detail and reveal that she had female sex organs!*

It's sometimes very hard to spot the queen in the middle of 50,000 other bees, even with her longer body and larger legs. Many beekeepers put a small dot of paint on her back which makes it much easier to 'spot' her!

Honeybees store honey (top left) and pollen (right) in the wax cells.

Up the workers!

A worker bee works very hard throughout her lifetime (I'm sure you've heard the expression 'as busy as a bee'?). As she gets older her role changes. When she's born her first job is to clean out her cell. Imagine a newborn baby having to clean their own bedroom!

Duties of worker bees

- **1-2 days:** **Cleaner**: cleans cells ready for the next egg.
- **3-11 days:** **Nurse and care assistant**: feeds and looks after larvae.
- **12-17 days:** **Builder and undertaker**: produces wax, builds honeycomb, carries food and removes dead bees.
- **18-21 days:** **Security officer**: guards the hive entrance to stop other insects getting in.
- **22+ days:** **Food gatherer and cook**: pollinates plants, collects pollen, nectar and water and makes honey.

In the summer a worker bee only lives for about 40 days. As no young are raised over the winter months, worker bees born in the autumn will live until the following spring.

An average hive will contain around 50,000 bees in the summer but only about 10,000 in the winter.

Drone on

A male drone bee doesn't do any work and is really quite lazy, expecting the female worker bees to wait on him hand and foot! His only job is to mate with the queen. The drone bee has huge eyes to help him find the queen when she's flying high in the air. The fastest drones that successfully mate with the queen will die, as they lose their sex organs in the process.

Most of the time a drone bee sits around in the hive feasting on honey brought to him by the worker bees. Worker bees get their own back in the early autumn when they stop feeding the old drones.

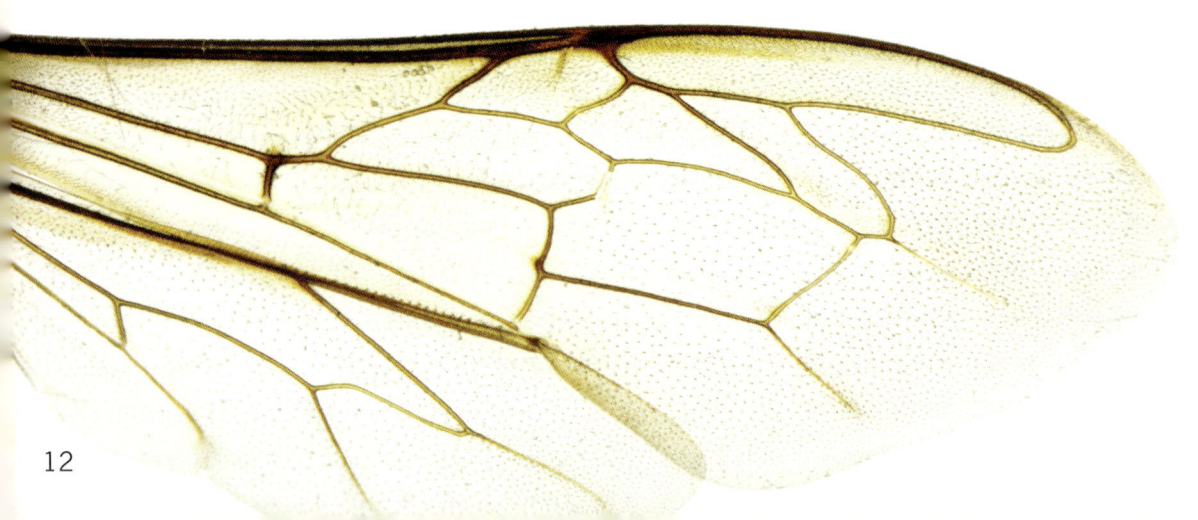

If they don't die from starvation, the worker bees kick the drones out of the hive and maybe even bite off their wings for good measure!

Above: it's a great life if you're a drone... until autumn arrives.

Left: a bee's wings flap around 230 times a second, creating quite a buzz!

Buzzwords: *A drone bee doesn't have a father... but he does have a grandfather. Think about it!*

Honeybees create wax honeycombs in wooden frames in modern hives.

Beehives come in all shapes, sizes and materials, depending on when and where they were made. Modern hives in the UK are simple wooden boxes.

14

A hive of activity

Home sweet home

Our special relationship with bees goes back a long time. About 15,000 years ago, a caveman artist painted a primitive picture on a cave wall in Spain which shows two men climbing up a tall ladder, basket in hand, out to steal a bees' nest. The artist even painted some angry bees buzzing around the hunter!

The Ancient Egyptians were probably the first people to keep bees in hives, though they looked quite different to the hives we use today. Honey was highly prized by the Egyptians and used in medicines and ointments and to dress wounds.

Beekeeping spread quickly throughout the ancient world. In Greece, Turkey and Iran, hives were built into walls. In heavily forested countries, hollowed out log hives were suspended from trees. In Spain and Portugal hives were made out of cork, while those in England, France and the Netherlands were made from wood or clay-covered straw. When America was colonised in the 17th century, the English settlers brought bees with them from England in 'skeps' made from coiled straw, the shape we traditionally associate with beehives.

Many modern hives are actually quite boring to look at - just a wooden box with a hole for the bees to fly in and out of. Inside, there's an upper level for storing the honey and a lower level where the queen lays her eggs and the young are reared.

Buzzwords: *The Babylonians, Ancient Greeks and Egyptians often embalmed their dead kings and war heroes in honey to preserve their bodies. Maybe that's how we get the expression 'the sweet smell of success'?*

First a larva, then a pupa; then a young adult. A bee develops the same way as this wasp.

Baby boom

As the queen is constantly laying eggs during the summer there are always baby bees in various stages of development in the hive.

All bees start life as an egg. Three days after being laid, the egg hatches into a larva. This looks a bit like a little grub. The larva is fed by the young worker bees for about five days on a rich diet called 'brood food' made in a bee's body from honey, pollen, nectar, saliva and enzymes. The larva develops into a pupa, which is kept warm in its own silky cocoon in a sealed cell in the honeycomb. Finally, after chewing its way out of its cocoon and wax cell, the young bee emerges (left).

Wax works

Beeswax comes from wax glands on the underbellies of young bees. Worker bees chew the flakes of wax and mould them with their legs into hexagonal cells to house their young and the honey they produce. To help make beeswax, bees eat lots of honey then huddle close together to raise their body temperature. They need to eat about 4.5kg (10lbs) of honey to produce 454g (1lb) of wax.

Shape shifters

Cells in a honeycomb are almost round... but not quite. Honeybees shape the cells into six-sided hexagons which fit together really well and make best use of the limited space in the hive.

Some like it hot

When the hive gets too hot in the summer, bees have developed their own special kind of air-conditioning! Worker bees fly off and collect water to spread around inside the hive. Then several rows of bees around the entrance to the hive fan their wings in time together, creating a cool draught!

Baby it's cold outside!

When it's cold, bees snuggle up closely together and shake their bodies to generate heat. They take turns being on the colder, outer edges of the group. A winter bee colony looks very different to a summer one. There may only be 5,000–10,000 worker bees and a queen, with no drones, surviving on the stored honey in the hive until the flowers blossom again in spring.

Flower power

Bees are specialised insects called pollinators that gather nectar and pollen from flowers. As pollinators, they are vital to our food chain, helping plants to reproduce. In the UK, about 70 crops are pollinated by bees. Bees also pollinate the flowers of many other plants that are fed to farm animals. One third of the food we eat would not be available if it wasn't for the hard-working bees!

Farmers in some parts of the world actually pay beekeepers to put hives in their fields and orchards, as crops grow better when they are well pollinated.

Food glorious food!

Pollen is a well-balanced food with almost all of the essential nutrients bee larvae need to grow and survive. Worker bees have a pollen 'basket' on the outside of their back legs made up of rows of stiff hairs that bend to form a hollow space. When a bee visits a flower, she combs grains of pollen into her baskets. Pollen from the flower also sticks to the bee's hair.

Bees can fly as far as five miles for food, but don't usually travel further than a mile or so from the hive. Worker bees fly at a top speed of around 15-20mph (21-28km/h) when flying to fetch food and about 12mph (17km/h) when coming back laden with nectar, pollen or water. A worker bee can visit up to 10,000 flowers in a day before she returns to the hive. After all this work she may only generate a teaspoonful of honey during her whole lifetime!

As well as seeking out nectar and pollen, bees sometimes collect a very sticky substance called propolis or 'bee glue', which comes from the buds of trees. They use this propolis to plug gaps in the hive, line egg cells, repair damaged honeycomb or cover up anything that shouldn't be in the hive, like a stray beetle or insect!

Tell 'em about the honey mummy

Bees have a long tongue like a straw that they use to suck up the sweet nectar from flowers. They store the nectar in the honey sac inside their body.

When the bees return to the hive they transfer the nectar into the mouths of the younger bees – it looks a bit like they are kissing! There it mixes with enzymes which help turn the nectar into honey. The young bees then deposit the nectar in cells and fan it by flapping their wings so that excess water evaporates.

When the honey's just right, the bees seal the cell with a thin layer of wax until they need it. This wax cap tells the beekeeper that the honey is ready to be harvested.

Buzzwords: *The only things sweeter in nature than honey are dates.*

Bee are vital to our food chain, helping plants to reproduce. One third of the food we eat would not be available if it wasn't for the hard-working bees!

Will you waggle dance with me?

Bees can't talk – the buzzing noise they make is caused by their wings rubbing together very fast. However, they have developed an amazing way to communicate with each other... by dancing! Better still, we humans have learned to understand what they are saying to each other.

A worker bee returning to the hive from a rich source of food dances around in a circle, then crosses it at a certain point. This tells the other bees the direction to travel to find the food. It's a bit like giving a compass bearing, but relative to the sun rather than magnetic north.

To pass on the distance from the hive, the bee 'waggles' its abdomen while crossing the circle... the more waggles, the greater the distance.

Sometimes the worker bees share the taste of the pollen and nectar to whet the other bees' appetites!

Making a beeline

Bees' eyes are more sensitive to the blue end of the colour spectrum. Flowers reflect large amounts of ultra violet light and to a bee will appear very bright... unless the flowers are red. Red flowers look dull and uninteresting to bees as they are totally red blind!

If you look closely at flowers you will see that many have bright markings and some have dark lines called honeylines to help guide bees to the nectar.

Sniffer bees go down a bomb

Honeybees have an amazing sense of smell. They know which flowers have the best nectar and pollen and they can recognise them just from their scent.

Scientists have actually made use of this skill to detect hidden explosives. They have invented a box containing three trained bees and a video camera. The bees react when they smell explosives... at concentrations as low as two parts per trillion. That's the same as finding a grain of sand in a swimming pool!

Sniffer bees have actually proved to be more effective than sniffer dogs. They are not so easily distracted, learn quicker and are cheaper to keep!

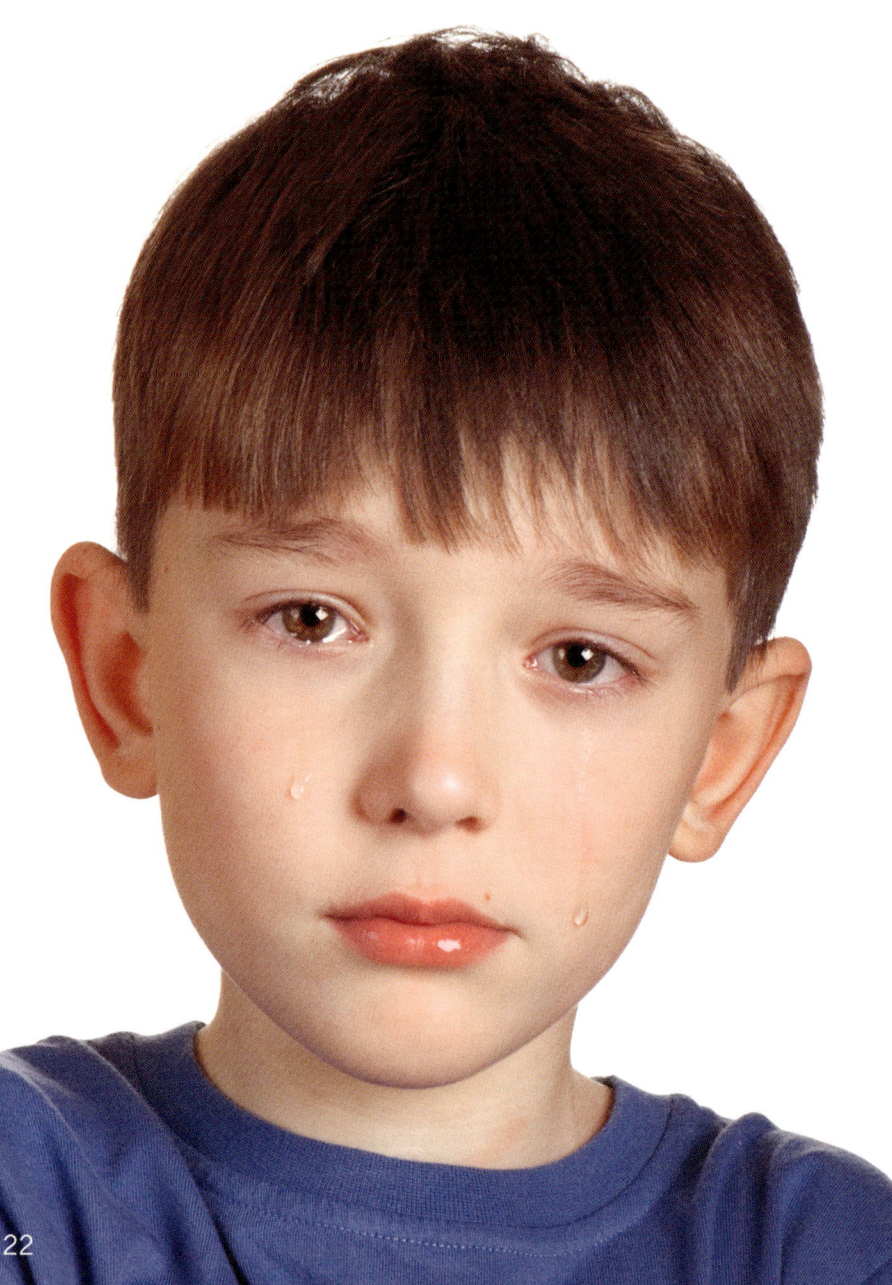

The sting in the tail

A bee usually stings for one of two reasons: to protect the hive or when frightened. If you find yourself near bees, move slowly. Don't wave your arms and leap around. The bees may think you are an enemy and try to sting you. If the bees get angry, walk away through undergrowth or trees if possible. If a bee lands on you, stand still and wait until it flies off. Don't try to swat it away.

Only worker bees can sting you – the queen only stings other queens! A bee sting has little barbs or hooks on it which cause it to stay firmly stuck in your skin. It continues to pump venom into you even after the bee has flown off, so it's best to remove the sting as soon as possible by scraping it off with a fingernail. When a bee stings it loses its venom sac and glands, causing it to die.

Some beekeepers claim bee stings are good for relieving pain from arthritis or rheumatism and, in Russia, bee stings are often used to treat people who have joint problems. However, bee stings can be very dangerous if you are allergic to them. They can cause your throat to swell up and sometimes can lead to death if not treated immediately.

Buzzwords: *The most stings anyone has received and survived to tell the tale is 2,243. Ouch!*

Warning — swarming!

Don't panic if you see a swarm of bees – they are usually in a good mood! They'll be stuffed with so much honey that they will actually find it quite hard to sting you. If the swarm is not causing a nuisance, leave it alone. The bees will cluster together and stay there while 'scout' bees look for a new home.

Your local council usually keeps a list of beekeepers who will come and collect the bees if they are being a nuisance. If the beekeeper puts a hive with some old honeycomb in it close by, it is quite easy to persuade the swarm to move in.

Buzzwords: *Bee 'beards' were popular in the 18th and 19th centuries. Entertainers would place the queen on their chin. The other bees follow her, creating an artificial swarm shaped like a beard!*

Rain, rain go away

Predicting the weather has challenged humans since the dawn of time. Today, highly sensitive measuring instruments, satellite pictures and instant electronic communication allow meteorologists to make accurate weather forecasts. But sometimes it's probably just as effective to look out of the window and see what the bees are doing!

Bees, like other insects, are very good at predicting the weather. They don't like getting caught in a shower, so when they sense that it might rain they never stray too far from the hive.

Sometimes bees seem to work doubly hard searching for food early in the day if they sense that it might rain later. When it does rain, they tend to stay in the dry in their hive. Very sensible!

Here's an old rhyme to help you to predict the weather:

When bees to distance wing their flight,
Days are warm and skies are bright.
But, when their flight ends near their home,
Stormy weather is sure to come.

Bee bounty

Honey

Honey can be hard or soft, nearly clear or dark brown. It has its own unique flavour, depending on the types of flowers and plants near the hive. Crops such as oil seed rape (you've probably seen the bright yellow fields in the spring) produce honey that sets very hard... so hard, in fact, that even bees find it difficult to use during a cold winter!

Some beekeepers like to produce honey made from one particular flower, such as clover, orange blossom or lavender, so the hive has to be carefully positioned to encourage the bees to feed only from those plants. This can be difficult, and most honey is usually a mix of different flowers. In the autumn, some beekeepers move their hives on to moors so that the bees can harvest the nectar from wild heather. Heather honey is said to be the 'king' of honeys.

Mead

Before people discovered how to brew beer and make wine, they fermented honey with water and yeast to make the first alcoholic drink – mead. Some people call it the 'Nectar of the Gods'. Others think it tastes like cough mixture... ugh!

Buzzwords: Archaeologists found 3,000-year-old honeycombs in the tombs of the Egyptian Pharaohs... and the honey in them was still edible!

It's possible that the secret of how to make this honey wine was discovered accidentally by Stone Age man, perhaps when honey became wet from rain and wild yeast settled into the mixture.

An old European custom had newly-married couples drink honey wine for a whole moon (month) to increase their chances of having children and therefore of enjoying a long and happy marriage. That's how we get the word 'honeymoon'. Some people drink mead now as a health drink, as it contains a lot of the goodness of honey.

Royal Jelly

Royal Jelly is very rich in proteins and fatty acids. Some people claim that it has almost 'magical' health properties! You can buy it in health food shops but it's very expensive, even though some products only contain about 2% of the real thing.

Bee bread

Bee bread is a mixture of plant pollen and honey, which bees mould into granules and store in their honeycombs. Plant pollen can make you sneeze and have a runny nose and eyes if you are allergic to it, but some people believe that eating bee bread can actually help prevent that happening.

Many Olympic athletes eat bee bread, as they believe it strengthens their immune system, increases oxygen intake, boosts performance and helps them recover quicker after training.

Early Egyptians and the ancient Chinese considered bee bread to have amazing healing properties and called it the 'Fountain of Youth' and 'Ambrosia of the Gods'.

Left: Not to everyone's taste, but mead was the world's first alcoholic drink.
Right: Plant pollen collected by bees, which they make into 'bee bread'.

Beeswax

Candles made from beeswax give off a honey-scented glow and burn cleanly and brightly. But beeswax can be found in many other products, including soap, skin care products, the coatings of sweets (like jellybeans), pills and cheese, crayons and polish. Some honey lovers like to chew it like gum!

Buzzwords: *Madame Tussaud started her lifelong interest in waxwork models when she was asked to make death masks of King Louis XVI and his wife, Marie Antoinette. The Royal couple had their heads chopped off during the French Revolution in the late 18th century!*

Harvesting the honey

Beekeepers remove the surplus honey from their hives twice a year in the UK. The bees don't miss it too much... a strong colony can produce 2-3 times more honey than it needs. If necessary, beekeepers feed their bees with sugar syrup in the autumn if there is a shortage of nectar.

The upper frames in the hive where honey is stored are called 'supers'. The queen bee is kept out of there by a wire or plastic grid called a queen excluder. This only allows the smaller worker bees to pass through. During the summer, the beekeeper adds more supers until it's time to harvest the honey.

The beekeeper then replaces the queen excluder with a special one-way flap which stops all the bees getting to the honeycombs. When all the bees are trapped in the lower part of the hive, the beekeeper can lift out the supers containing the honeycombs. Beekeepers usually wear protective clothes, gloves, hat and veil so they don't get stung. Their clothes are white, which calms the bees.

After removing the wax cappings from the cells, the honeycombs are spun round at high speed in a spinner to extract all the honey. This is then filtered to remove any large bits of pollen, propolis and wax before being poured into glass jars. One hive can produce about 27kg (60lb) or more of honey in a good season. However, on average, it's usually around 14 kg (30lb).

Buzzwords: *Bees fly about 55,000 miles to make just one pound (454g) of honey... that's one and a half times around the world!*

Smoke screen

If bees get scared they release a special smell that warns other bees that they are in danger. When a beekeeper opens up a hive he puffs in smoke to cover up the alarm smell and calm the bees.

Bees are woodland insects and evolution has taught them to fear fire more than anything else. When bees sense smoke they try and eat as much honey as possible in case they have to abandon the hive quickly. This distracts them while the beekeeper removes the honeycombs.

Bees are an endangered species!

Bees' survival is very important to us. You may not have noticed it, but there has been a huge decline in the number of bees in the past few years.

Parasites, pesticides, habitat loss and new farming methods have all helped to significantly reduce the number of bees.

Parasites are the main reason bees are endangered. Varroa mites reproduce inside hive cells where young bees are being raised and can spread harmful viruses and diseases. Tracheal mites live inside the windpipe (trachea) of bees and suck their blood from the inside.

Wherever possible, beekeepers use natural products and management techniques to control these parasites, as they can become resistant to chemical treatments. Some beekeepers are even trying to breed new types of bee that are more resistant to mites.

A lot of native bees' natural habitats are rapidly disappearing, as we try and make room for the world's growing population. Changes in the way crops are grown and the increasing use of pesticides have also reduced the number of flowering plants that bees need to thrive.

The good news is, many farmers are now leaving conservation strips around the edges of their fields, which can encourage the growth of bee-friendly plants.

How YOU can help

Plant bee-friendly plants
Honeybees love most herbs, daisy-shaped flowers and fruit trees, so be sure to grow these in your garden. The best flowers for attracting bees are usually yellow, blue and purple.

Be kind to bees
Bees only sting when annoyed or frightened. If you see a bee, or feel scared around bees, stay calm and walk away slowly.

Protect swarms
If you see a bee swarm, contact your local council. They will arrange for a beekeeper to collect it. Swarms are not usually dangerous, but you can make the bees aggressive if you disturb them or spray them with water.

Avoid using pesticides
Some pesticides can harm bees. Try and use safe, organic products in your garden.

Wash your old honey jars
Honey from other countries can contain bacteria and spores that are very harmful to our honeybees. If bees eat the leftover honey they can become infected, which could kill off the whole hive. Always wash out honey jars thoroughly and dispose of them carefully.

Find space for a hive
Many beekeepers are looking for places to site their hives and will be pleased to show you inside. If you have a hive in your garden, vegetables will grow better, fruit trees will produce more fruit and your garden will be buzzing with life!

Learn more about this fascinating insect
See if there are any beekeeping groups near you or events you can attend. You can find out lots about bees from the British Beekeepers Association (see page 35 for contact details).

Become a beekeeper
You will need to spend at least £300 on a basic second hand hive, clothing, tools and a starter colony of bees from a local beekeeper. However, you should learn all about keeping bees first, and you will need an adult to supervise you if you are under 18. Many beekeeping associations have young people's groups.

Bee recipes

Honey muffins

Ingredients
150g of self-raising flour
½ teaspoonful of bicarbonate of soda
½ teaspoonful of salt
100g of brown sugar
50g of toasted wheat bran
75g of raisins
120ml of boiling water
75g of unsalted butter or margarine
60ml of honey
120ml of milk
1 large egg, beaten

Preheat the oven to 200° C (gas mark 6). Line twelve muffin cups with muffin papers or grease them well. Stir together the flour, bicarbonate of soda, salt and sugar. Put the bran and raisins in another bowl and mix in the boiling water. Meanwhile, melt the butter and honey together in a large saucepan. Allow to cool a bit then stir in the milk and beaten egg. Carefully fold in the flour mix and add the bran and dried fruit. Divide the mixture between the muffin cases and bake for about 15–20 minutes or until a skewer inserted into a muffin comes out clean.

'Honeycomb'

Ingredients
4 tablespoonfuls of golden syrup
1 tablespoonful of water
200g of caster sugar
3 teaspoonfuls of bicarbonate of soda

Grease a 20cm square cake tin or slice tray. In a large saucepan, heat the golden syrup and sugar together, bring to the boil then simmer on a low heat for 5–10 minutes. Cooking time will vary but test by dropping a little of the syrup into water – it should become brittle when ready. Watch it doesn't burn! Remove the saucepan from the heat and add the bicarbonate of soda. Mix it in quickly because the mixture will foam up instantly. Pour immediately into the cake tin. Leave to set then break into bite size chunks.

Tip: Make your own 'Crunchie' by dipping the pieces of honeycomb in melted chocolate, then letting them set on a piece of greaseproof paper.

Honey ice-cream

Ingredients
500ml of double cream
250ml of whole milk
1 vanilla pod
150ml of set honey

Split open the vanilla pod and scrape the seeds and inside of the pod into a large saucepan. Pour in the cream and milk and bring them just to the boil. Remove from the heat and stir in the honey until it has completely dissolved. Cover the saucepan with a lid and leave the mixture to cool. When it has cooled, strain it to remove the vanilla pod and pour it into a jug or bowl. Cover with clingfilm and chill in the fridge for at least an hour. Then churn it in an ice-cream maker, or freeze it in a shallow container in the freezer, whisking every now and then to break up the ice crystals.

Honey mustard salad dressing

Ingredients
2 tablespoonfuls of balsamic vinegar
1 teaspoonful of Dijon mustard
1 teaspoonful of honey
1 clove of garlic, finely chopped
1 shallot, finely chopped
¼ teaspoonful of salt
¼ teaspoonful of freshly ground black pepper

Whisk all ingredients together in a small bowl or shake in a jam jar to combine. Cover and keep in a fridge for up to one week.

Honey milk shake

Ingredients
Glass of milk
1 scoop of vanilla ice cream
2 teaspoonfuls of honey
Half a banana (optional)

Place the milk, ice cream and honey in a liquidiser or food processor. Whisk together until smooth and pour into a glass. Top with banana slices.

Honey pancakes

Ingredients
A stack of your favourite pancakes or waffles
Honey

Take your stack of warm pancakes or waffles. Pour over honey.

Erm… that's it!

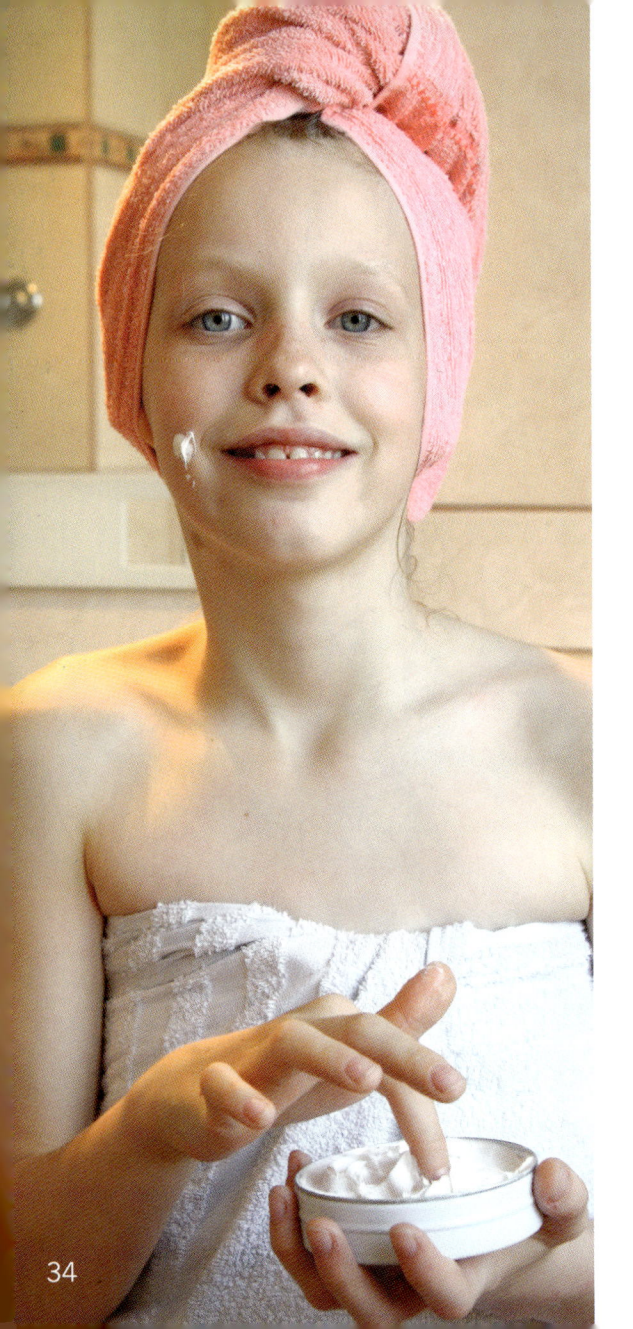

You may need an adult to help you with the next two recipes as hot wax can burn!

Lip balm

Ingredients
2 tablespoonfuls of grated beeswax
4 teaspoonfuls of almond oil
2 teaspoonfuls of honey

Place all the ingredients in a glass bowl over a saucepan of simmering water. When everything has completely melted, remove from the heat, stir together and pour into small containers. Wait for the mixture to cool before putting the lids on (and using!).

Body moisturiser cream (*good for wind and sunburned skin*)

Ingredients
2 tablespoonfuls of beeswax
2 teaspoonfuls of distilled water
115g of cocoa butter
4 tablespoonfuls of sweet almond oil
2 tablespoonfuls of coconut oil

Carefully melt the beeswax in a saucepan over a low heat with the water. Add in the cocoa butter a spoonful at a time and stir. Gradually add the other oils. Pour into a glass jar and wait for the mixture to cool before putting the lid on.

Beeswax candles

Ingredients
Beeswax candle wax (usually sold in 25cm x 30cm or 35cm x 40cm sheets)
Candle wicks

Beeswax is a fairly soft wax and can be easily moulded at room temperature. Lay a sheet of beeswax on a clean, flat surface with the 'width' edge towards you. Cut the wick about 5cm longer than this edge. Place the wick along the edge of the sheet closest to you and gently press it into the wax. Slowly roll the sheet up tightly around the wick, taking care not to trap air between the layers. When you have finished rolling the candle, gently press the edge of the wax sheet to seal the seam. Trim the wick at the bottom of the completed candle and leave about 1cm at the other end ready to light.